Life at Home

Simon Rose

Weigl

Published by Weigl Educational Publishers Limited
6325 – 10 Street SE
Calgary, Alberta, Canada
T2H 2Z9

Website: www.weigl.ca

Library and Archives Canada Cataloguing in Publication

Rose, Simon, 1961-, author
     Life at home / Simon Rose.

(Canada in World War I)
Includes index.
Issued in print and electronic formats.
ISBN 978-1-77071-243-0 (bound).--ISBN 978-1-77071-244-7 (pbk.).--
ISBN 978-1-77071-245-4 (epub)

     1. Canada--History--1914-1918--Juvenile literature. 2. World War,
1914-1918--Canada--Juvenile literature. I. Title.

FC557.R68 2013   j971.061   C2013-904315-2
                                                  C2013-904316-0

Printed in the United States of America
1 2 3 4 5 6 7 8 9 0 17 16 15 14 13

072013
WEP130613

We acknowledge the financial support of the Government of Canada
through the Canada Book Fund for our publishing activities.

Photograph and Text Credits
Alamy: pages 8, 9, 11, 17, 18, 19, 20, 23, 24, 26; Dreamstime: page 9;
Edwina Suley, Carbonear Heritage Society, Newfoundland, Canada,
page 23 (Clara Hawker); Getty Images: pages 4, 5, 6, 7, 8, 9, 10, 12, 13,
14, 15, 16, 18, 22, 25, 27, 28; Library and Archives Canada: page 22;
McCord Museum: page 21

Every reasonable effort has been made to trace ownership and to
obtain permission to reprint copyright material. The publishers
would be pleased to have any errors or omissions brought to their
attention so that they may be corrected in subsequent printings.

Senior Editor
Aaron Carr

Art Director
Terry Paulhus

Life at Home

CONTENTS

Young men and even boys joined the military to fight in the war. This left many jobs vacant.

With a shortage of work at home, many Canadians were eager to join the war effort.

The Halifax Explosion of 1917 destroyed most of the city.

ATTENDRONS-NOUS QUE LES NÔTRES BRÛLENT?

ENRÔLONS-NOUS et tout de suite

Dans Le 178ième

Bataillon CANADIEN FRANÇAIS

Commandé par le Lt.Col.Girouard et six autres officiers du 22ième tous de retour du Front.

INFORMATIONS AUX QUARTIERS OU COIN St ANDRÉ ET St

Posters played a very important role in Canada's efforts to raise funds for the war.

The War Begins

Many women worked in factories during the war.

Most of World War I was fought in Europe, but the conflict had a lasting impact in Canada as well. The economy developed, and people's lives were affected as the war brought great social and political change. With men serving overseas in the armed forces, women began entering the workforce. Men returned to their jobs after the war, but the role of women in society had changed. The fight for women's **suffrage** had existed before the war and continued during the conflict. In 1918, women in Canada won the right to vote.

When the war was over, large numbers of soldiers returned home in a short period of time. This led to the creation of programs to assist soldiers and their families. These programs laid the foundation for the systems of social welfare and healthcare that Canada would adopt over the next few decades.

The government took more control of the economy during the war years. **Income tax** had been introduced to help pay for the war, but it later became permanent. Many of the measures the government undertook during the war were used again during World War II. These measures included the control of important industries, recruiting women into the workforce, **conscription** of men into the armed forces, and mobilizing the people and economy for wartime conditions.

As a result of World War I, Canada's position on the world stage was greatly enhanced. When the war ended, Canada was represented at the peace conference and signed the **Treaty of Versailles** separately from Great Britain. Canada was on its way to becoming a fully independent country.

Theatre of War

I n 1914, Canada was a self-governing **dominion** of the British Empire. This meant that the Canadian government looked after its own affairs and was not directly ruled by Great Britain. Though Canada and Newfoundland were automatically at war with Germany and its allies as soon as Great Britain declared war in August 1914, Canada had a say in its level of involvement. The Canadian government decided what the country's contribution to the war effort would be.

Canada became a country in 1867. The provinces of Saskatchewan and Alberta were created in 1905. When the war began, Newfoundland was a separate British **colony**. Canada had a population of about 3.5 million in 1867. This had grown to almost 8 million by 1914, largely as a result of immigration. Most Canadians lived in Ontario and Quebec, but the population was growing in the western provinces.

Canada and Newfoundland, 1914–1918

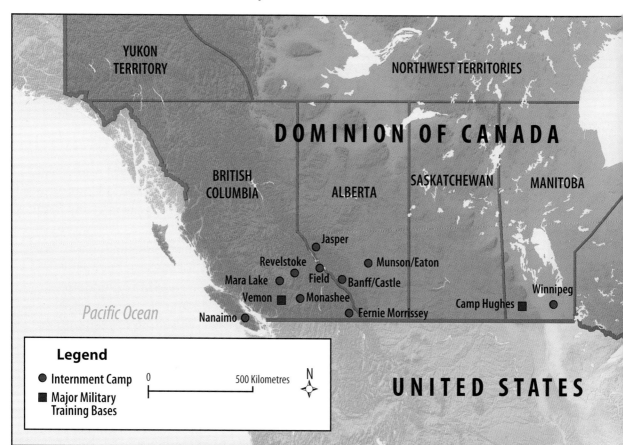

The Liberal party had been in charge of the Canadian government during the previous decade, but in 1911, Robert Borden led the Conservative party to victory in the general election. There were tensions between English and French Canadians, and women were campaigning for the right to vote in provincial and federal elections. Women also wanted to be allowed to run for political office.

In the years before 1914, Canada had the world's fastest-growing economy. The Canadian Pacific Railway had been completed in 1885, linking the country from coast to coast. In the west, farmers grew wheat and other crops, which were transported by rail to the east. Some farm products were then exported to Europe. In May 1914, oil had been discovered in Alberta. This discovery would transform the economy of the western provinces. The economy grew more slowly in the Atlantic Provinces, but in Central Canada, the decades prior to World War I saw a period of increasing industrialization. Though Canada still traded with Great Britain, the country also had trading relationships with the United States and the countries of the Caribbean, Central America, and South America.

Sir Robert Borden (1854–1937)

Robert Borden was born in 1854 in Grand-Pré, Nova Scotia. After completing his education, he became a teacher, working at first in Nova Scotia and later in the United States. When Borden returned to Canada, he became a lawyer. By 1890, he was the head of a law firm in Halifax.

In 1896, Borden was elected to the House of Commons. He became the leader of the Conservative party in 1901. Borden spent the next 10 years rebuilding the party and won the 1911 federal election. Borden served as prime minister during World War I and helped Canada play a larger role on the world stage. He was prime minister until health problems led to his resignation in 1920. Borden died in Ottawa in 1937.

June 28 - Archduke Franz Ferdinand, heir to the throne of Austria-Hungary, is assassinated in Sarajevo.

August 3 - Germany declares war on France.

FOR KING AND COUNTRY

August 4 - Great Britain declares war on Germany. Canada and Newfoundland are members of the British Empire and are now at war, too.

October 3 - The first members of the Canadian Expeditionary Force sail for Great Britain.

December 21 - Princess Patricia's Canadian Light Infantry is the first Canadian unit to arrive in France.

April 22 to 25 - At the Second Battle of Ypres, Canadian troops are attacked with poison gas.

February 21 - Nellie McClung presents a petition in the Alberta Legislature seeking the vote for women.

May 7 - A **U-boat** sinks the ocean liner *Lusitania*, killing almost 1,200 people, including many Canadians and Americans.

January - In Manitoba, women win the right to vote and hold political office in the province.

March - Women gain the vote in Saskatchewan.

April - Women win the right to vote in Alberta.

July 1 to November 18 - Soldiers from Canada and Newfoundland are heavily involved in the Battle of the Somme.

September - Citizens of Berlin, Ontario, officially change the town's name to Kitchener.

November - Sir Samuel Hughes resigns from his position as the minister of militia and defense.

Canada played one of the most important roles of all British Empire countries during World War I.

April - Women win the right to vote in both Ontario and British Columbia.

April 9 to 17 - Canadian soldiers defeat the Germans at Vimy Ridge.

August - The Military Service Act is passed, allowing the government to conscript men into the armed forces if necessary.

September - Income tax is introduced to help finance the Canadian war effort.

September - The Wartime Elections Act grants the vote to women in the armed forces and the wives, widows, mothers, and sisters of soldiers fighting overseas.

Your Chums are fighting
Why aren't YOU?

October 26 to November 10 - Canada suffers more than 16,000 casualties in the Battle of Passchendaele.

December 6 - The Halifax Explosion kills 1,900 people when the *Mont Blanc*, a French ship carrying explosives, explodes in Halifax harbour.

December 17 - Robert Borden's **Unionists**, comprising both Conservatives and Liberals, win the federal election.

January -The conscription law in Canada begins to be enforced by the government.

April - Anti-conscription riots take place in Quebec City.

May 24 - All female citizens aged 21 and over are given the right to vote in federal elections in Canada.

August 8 to November 11 - Canadian troops fight in many battles during the Hundred Days Offensive

November 11 - The war comes to an end at the 11 a.m..

World War I caused great change throughout the world. Many empires in Europe ceased to exist. The North American countries of Canada and the United States began to grow as international powers.

Preparing for Battle

When World War I began in 1914, most Canadians expected the conflict to be short and not that expensive. Yet the war went on for much longer than expected, and costs continued to rise. The Canadian government had to take steps to organize the war effort.

Canada became a major centre for Allied war production, especially for artillery shells. In 1915, the Imperial **Munitions** Board (IMB) was created to oversee production of shells. The IMB was controlled by Great Britain but run by a Canadian. The IMB established state-owned factories to build munitions and also looked after the manufacture of ships and aircraft. Professional managers ran the operations, and more than 30,000 women were hired for jobs in factories and offices. By 1917, almost one-third of all British shells were being manufactured in Canada. The IMB expanded into the production of many different kinds of war materials and developed airfields for a large-scale Allied training program for pilots.

The Canadian Food Board created the Soldiers of the Soil (SOS) program. This encouraged teenage boys to volunteer to work on farms. By the end of the war, thousands of young men were helping farmers. The Ontario government also set up an agricultural program called the Farm Service Corps, which mostly recruited women. These women helped farmers, too. They helped pick fruit and did other work around farms.

Early in the war, the government simply asked the public to use less fuel or produce more food to help the war effort. In the summer of 1917, however, the government appointed controllers to manage production, waste, and shortages of fuel and food. The Board of Grain Supervisors managed wheat prices. The Canada Food Board licensed and monitored food sales in restaurants and suggested alternatives for high-demand ingredients. Newspapers published special "war menus" to help families to conserve food. Municipal and provincial governments regulated local power use. They sometimes closed factories or schools for short periods of time to save energy.

The organization of the war effort had long-lasting effects. The lessons that the government learned from managing the Canadian economy from 1914 to 1918 would be of great help during World War II, 21 years later.

With so many men fighting in Europe, Canadian farms suffered from labour shortages.

In Canada, food clubs were started to collect food for the troops.

Most Canadian soldiers received their first training at Valcartier, Quebec.

Training helped prepare soldiers for daily life during the war.

Many women found new freedom working outside the home.

Recruiting new soldiers was a constant job.

War Materials

Canada sent hundreds of thousands of soldiers to fight in World War I. It also supplied food and weapons for the Allies. Hundreds of Canadian factories helped produce weapons, ammunition, ships, and aircraft for the Allied war effort.

Shells

Canada was located far from the battlefields in Europe, so it could manufacture products in relative safety. In 1914, Canada had virtually no munitions industry. By the end of the war, however, it was producing millions of artillery shells in factories all over the country. In 1916 alone, Canada shipped almost 20 million shells. During the course of the war, more than 66 million shells were produced in Canadian factories for the Allied armies.

Fuses

Fuses were an important part of shell manufacturing. The fuse allowed the shell to explode in the air after a time delay or explode on impact. The gunner at the front line set the time delay before the shell was fired. In factories, inspectors used special instruments to check the fuses before they were shipped out. If the fuses were not made correctly, the time delay would not be set properly. The shell could then explode before it was fired, with disastrous consequences for the soldiers.

Ships

Ships were needed for the Allied navies and for the merchant marine that transported weapons and foodstuffs. German U-boats in the Atlantic sank many ships and these needed to be replaced quickly. Great Britain built its own ships, but Canada helped. Large numbers of merchant ships and naval vessels were manufactured in Canada's industrial plants. By 1918, Canada had built more than 103 naval vessels..

Aircraft

The airplane had been invented in the early 1900s and was used for the first time in large-scale combat during World War I. Canada not only built planes for the war effort, but it also developed airfields for pilot training programs. In World War I, men from all over the world arrived to train in Canada in a safe environment. The Imperial Air Schools trained pilots and helped prepare them for aerial combat in Europe. More than 2,600 aircraft were built in Canada during the war.

Natural Resources

Canada's natural resources were also essential to the war effort. Copper, lead, and nickel were exported from Canada to many European countries and used in war production at home. Canadian lumber was also in great demand throughout the war. This growing demand for resources greatly increased Canada's industrial output. Before 1914, Canada had exported most of the country's raw materials to the United States. During the war, industries that used these raw materials began to develop in Canada. This created more jobs for Canadians.

Food

Canadian farmers supplied Great Britain and other Allied armies with great amounts of foodstuffs in World War I. The result was a tremendous boost to the Canadian economy. The demand for foodstuffs benefited western Canada's farmers as grain prices increased during the war. Canada exported grain, beef, canned fish, and many other products to its allies in Europe.

DO YOUR BIT

SAVE FOOD

Role of the Government

Governments controlled sensitive military information during wartime. During World War I, soldiers' letters home from the front were read by censors and edited if necessary. In Canada, official censors monitored newspapers and magazines to check if any of the content could damage the war effort. Editors and publishers could be sent to prison if they ignored warnings about what they were publishing.

To generate support for the war, the government also produced large amounts of **propaganda**. Posters were printed with many different themes, though most were designed to encourage people to join the armed forces. Other posters reminded people of the reasons why the war was being fought, either by depicting the enemy in an unfavourable way or by praising Canada and the rest of the British Empire. There were posters asking people to contribute to charities or work hard to **ration** scarce supplies of fuel or food. Rallies and parades also took place, some of which tried to shame those considered not to be supporting the war effort. Many posters encouraged people to buy **Victory Bonds.**

To help raise money for the war, some posters encouraged Canadians to buy war bonds. This money went to the government.

Conscription

In August 1914, no one expected the conflict to last long. Though there was plenty of enthusiasm to join the armed forces when the war began, as more and more men were killed or wounded, fewer men were enlisting. The government had wanted to avoid forcing men to join the army, but in 1917 it introduced conscription to maintain Canada's troop levels. The Conscription Crisis deeply divided Canadians. Many farmers, unionized workers, French-Canadians, and non-British immigrants opposed conscription. English-speaking Canadians, British immigrants, older Canadians, and the families of soldiers were generally in favour of it.

> "We heard the thud of hooves of an Ontario cavalry regiment, driven at breakneck speed into rue Saint Sauveur. Rioters had put out the street lamps; the Lower City was shrouded in mist and darkness that night. Suddenly, I could make out the fire of several heavy machine guns. It was deafening and gave the impression that a massacre was taking place at the foot of the cliff."
>
> *Frank Scott, a soldier on leave in Quebec City during an anti-conscription riot, April 1, 1918*

Farmers in western Canada knew how important they were to the war effort and resented their sons being forced into the army, creating a labour shortage on the farms. In many parts of Canada, workers felt that ordinary people were suffering from the effects of inflation and were being killed overseas, while some businesspeople were getting rich from the war. French-Canadian men had been among the first to enlist in 1914, but they later began to feel that the war was just helping Great Britain expand its empire.

Conscription was an issue in many countries, including Ireland.

The Military Service Act was introduced in Parliament, and there were fierce debates throughout the summer of 1917 before it passed in August. All male citizens between 20 and 45 years of age became subject to military service, if called up, for the rest of the war. Some men were exempt from the law if their jobs were essential to the war effort or if their families would be badly affected if they joined the armed forces.

Conscription was the main issue in the federal election in December 1917. Many English-speaking Liberals joined Prime Minister Robert Borden's Conservatives, and together they fought the campaign as Unionists. Borden also introduced laws that helped him win the election. The Wartime Elections Act gave the vote to the wives, mothers, and sisters of soldiers, who were mostly in favour of conscription. The Act also took the right to vote away from people considered **enemy aliens**, unless they had a family member in the armed forces. The Military Voters Act gave the vote to all military personnel and nurses, who also mostly supported conscription. Borden won the election, capturing more than 90 percent of the votes from the armed forces.

Despite conscription becoming law, opposition and protests continued. During Easter 1918, there were riots and street battles in Quebec City over the conscription issue. Four people were killed and many injured in the disturbances. About 120,000 Canadian men were eventually conscripted. By the time the war ended in November 1918, however, only 48,000 had been shipped to Europe. Of those sent overseas, only about half actually served at the front.

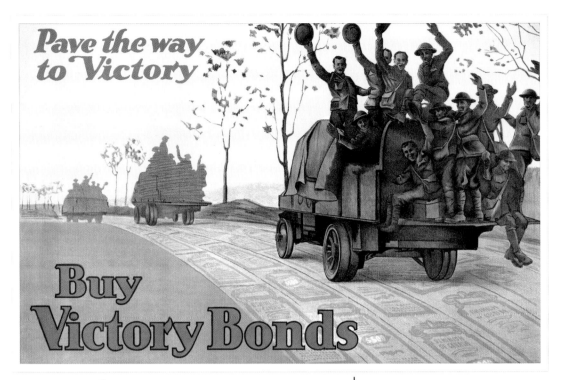

Pave the way to Victory

Buy Victory Bonds

On the Home Front

Many posters depicted brave individuals or glorious victories to inspire people to buy war bonds.

The cost of World War I put a great strain on Canada's financial resources. The government set regulations to control the supply of resources and also rationed or set quotas for many everyday items that were considered important to the war effort. To raise revenue, wartime savings bonds were issued, and special wartime taxes were introduced.

Building materials, food, and gasoline, along with many other items, were all rationed during the war. People were allowed to buy only certain amounts of these things. This was meant to ensure that important supplies would not run out. To earn money for the war effort, customs duties were raised and luxury products, such as alcohol and tobacco, were taxed. In 1915, new taxes were placed on some food items, including tea, coffee, and sugar. Railway tickets, money orders, cheques, telegrams, and some medicines were also taxed, and postal rates were increased.

IF YOU CANNOT PUT THE "I" INTO FIGHT

YOU CAN PUT THE "PAY" INTO PATRIOTISM BY GIVING TO THE CANADIAN PATRIOTIC FUND

THE CANADIAN PATRIOTIC FUND

HIS MONTHLY GIFT

Besides government war bonds, private funds were also set up to raise money for the war effort.

In 1916, the Canadian government began taxing the incomes of large corporations with the Business Profits War Tax Act. The following year, the Canadian government introduced income tax for the first time. Canada had no income tax before World War I, which helped the country to attract new immigrants. The cost of the war left the government with little choice, however. Some people were exempt from the new tax, such as married Canadians earning less than $2,000 or unmarried Canadians with an income less than $1,000. The Income War Tax Act of 1917 was supposed to be temporary to help out the government, but income tax still exists today. Almost all working Canadians are taxed on their earnings.

Prince Arthur, the son of Queen Victoria, was the governor general of Canada. He spent much of his time supporting the war effort.

The Canadian Patriotic Fund

At the start of World War I, there were already private Canadian organizations that raised funds to support soldiers and their families, during and after wars. In August 1914, Sir Herbert Ames established the **Canadian Patriotic Fund** (CPF). This was a private organization, but it also had government support. The CPF raised almost $50 million for soldiers' families during the war, distributing financial assistance through a large volunteer network.

The CPF and other private groups were a great help in World War I, but most Canadians came to believe that the government should help to support the families of soldiers. In World War II, the federal government looked after soldiers and their families. This was an important step toward the creation of Canada's welfare system.

"The prompt and generous response on each occasion proves how truly Canada appreciates the duty which she owes to her sons who are fighting, for the Empire. … The Dominion is as determined as ever to … help the families of those who are serving in the Army and in the Navy."

Prince Arthur, governor general of Canada, asking for the public to support the Canadian Patriotic Fund, August 1914

Women at War

Most of the Canadians who served overseas during World War I were men. Women usually enlisted as nurses. However, women played a large role on the home front. Canadian women volunteered to knit and sew items that could be shipped to soldiers serving in Europe. Women made flannel shirts, pillows, scarves, sheets, and socks that were sent to the troops. Women founded many organizations and fundraising groups. For example, the Canadian Women's Hospital Ship Fund organized events, raising money for the war effort.

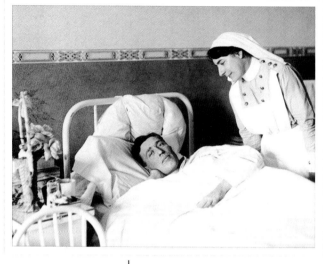

More than 3,000 Canadian nurses volunteered to serve in the war.

The war went on for much longer than anyone had expected, and more and more men joined the armed forces. Fewer people were available at home to work in jobs that were vital to Canada's economy. People were also needed to work in industries that provided materials for the country's war effort. Women started to take jobs that had previously always been done by men. Before 1914, some occupations were considered too difficult for women, such as driving buses and trucks, welding, or other industrial work. However, men were needed in the military, and since these jobs still needed to be done, women filled them instead. In Canada's war materials factories, around 12 percent of workers were female by 1917. When the war ended, more than 30,000 Canadian women were working in munitions factories. Many more worked in banks and offices or on farms with organizations such as the Farm Service Corps in Ontario.

"These girls all came from good homes and were all anxious to do their "bit." … In the factory we worked for ten and sometimes twelve hours a day, enlivening the monotony of the work by "making up" parodies to popular songs and telling stories to one another. Twelve of us at the first table christened ourselves the "family," and became the liveliest in the camp, and also some of the best workers."

Lois Allen, factory worker, 1918

Canadian women had been campaigning for suffrage, or the right to vote in elections, since the 1880s. Women such as Nellie McClung were leading figures in the movement for equal rights for women in the years before World War I. In 1916, McClung's efforts helped gain women the right to vote and to run for public office in Manitoba and Alberta.

Statues of Nellie McClung and four of the other women leaders involved in the suffrage movement, together known as the Famous Five, were placed on Parliament Hill in Ottawa, Ontario, in 2000.

The freedom women experienced in the workforce during the war made more women want to play a larger role in governing the country. Some politicians, including Prime Minister Robert Borden, were sympathetic, and there were many debates in Parliament. In 1918, Canadian women 21 years of age and older were given the right to vote in federal elections, though this did not apply to Asian and Aboriginal women at the time.

Nellie McClung 1873-1951

In 1973, a stamp was issued to commemorate Nellie McClung's birth in 1873 in Ontario.

The Enemy Within

When World War I began in August 1914, the **War Measures Act** was introduced. This allowed the federal government to limit or completely suspend **civil liberties** to protect the country. This included the right to imprison people living in Canada who were considered enemy aliens. These were citizens of countries that were now at war with Canada. At the start of the war, around 500,000 people living in Canada had been born in either Germany or Austria-Hungary. As the war progressed, people began to be suspicious of anyone who came from these countries or spoke their languages, thinking that they might be enemy agents. The federal government banned all publications and meetings in what were considered enemy languages. There was great hostility toward Germany in particular. This increased when a German U-boat sank the *Lusitania* in May 1915. Schools stopped teaching the German language. Sometimes, rioters attacked German-owned businesses and shops. The town of Berlin, Ontario, even changed its name to Kitchener in 1916. The local people did not want the town to have the same name as Germany's capital city.

Almost 1,200 people lost their lives when the *Lusitania* was sunk.

Anyone that the government thought might be an enemy agent was closely monitored. Around 80,000 people were required to carry identity cards and report to the police on a regular basis. Others were **interned** in camps all over the country. Between 1914 and 1920, 8,579 men connected to enemy countries were interned. Some of their dependents, including 81 women and 156 children, volunteered to join the men at the camps. Of those interned at camps across the country, 5,954 were Austro-Hungarians, 2,009 were Germans, 205 were Turks, and 99 were Bulgarians. The majority of people interned were of Ukrainian descent. At the time, much of Ukraine was part of Austria–Hungary, which was at war with Canada.

Many internment camps had barbed wire fences and armed guards.

Sir William Otter was in charge of the internment operation. His diaries record details of the administration and daily life at the camps. Internees worked in mining, logging, road and railway building, and on the development of Banff National Park. People sent to the camps had much of their money confiscated and were paid only about 25 cents per day, much less than other labourers at the time. Conditions could be harsh, especially in winter, and food was sometimes scarce or inadequate. Even when the war ended, some of the camps stayed in operation so that work projects could be completed.

"My dear father: We haven't nothing to eat and they do not want to give us no wood. My mother has to go four times to get something to eat. It is better with you, because we had everything to eat. This shack is no good, my mother is going down town every day and I have to go with her and I don't go to school at winter. It is cold in that shack. We your small children Kiss your hands my dear father. Goodbye my dear father. Come home right away."

Katie Domytryk in a letter to her father, who was interned at Spirit Lake in Quebec.

Leading Canadians

Sir Wilfrid Laurier (1841–1919)

Sir Wilfrid Laurier served as Canada's first French-Canadian prime minister from 1896 to 1911. He was also the leader of the Opposition in the House of Commons during World War I.

Laurier was born in 1841 in Saint-Lin, Canada East, which later became southern Quebec. After graduating from McGill University in 1864, he first became a lawyer and then went into business. Laurier was elected to the House of Commons in 1874. He became leader of the Liberal Party in 1889 and prime minister of Canada in 1896.

Laurier was defeated by Robert Borden's Conservative party in the election of 1911. He was a strong supporter of the war effort, but he opposed the introduction of conscription in 1917. The leading politician of his era, Laurier died in Ottawa in 1919.

Sir Herbert Brown Ames (1863–1954)

Sir Herbert Brown Ames was a businessman and politician. He was also well known as a **philanthropist**. During World War I, Ames was in charge of the Canadian Patriotic Fund.

Ames was born in Montreal, Quebec, in 1863. He graduated from Amherst College in 1885. Ames came from a wealthy family, and he used much of his wealth to improve the lives of the poor. He even built an apartment complex for those less fortunate.

Ames was a Conservative Member of Parliament from 1904 to 1920. When the war began in 1914, Ames set up the Canadian Patriotic Fund and served as its head. By March 31, 1917, the fund had raised nearly $23 million. The success of the fund was an inspiration to those who helped create social programs in Canada in the decades after World War I. He died in Montreal in 1954.

Sir Samuel Hughes (1853–1921)

Sir Samuel Hughes was Canada's minister of militia and defence from October 1911 to November 1916. He was the leading figure behind the country's war effort in the early years of World War I.

Hughes was born in 1853 near Bowmanville, Ontario. He attended the University of Toronto. Hughes served in the military in the 1860s and 1870s and was elected to the House of Commons in 1892. In 1911, Hughes became defence minister and led the Canadian war effort when the war began.

Hughes made sure the first Canadian troops were trained and ready to leave for Europe by early October 1914. By 1916, Hughes had become unpopular with his colleagues in the government. In November 1916, Hughes resigned from office, but he remained active in politics until his death in 1921.

Nellie McClung (1873–1951)

Nellie McClung was a feminist, politician, and activist in the early decades of the 20th century. She was active in the movements for social and political reform in western Canada and helped to secure full political rights for women.

McClung was born as Nellie Mooney in Ontario in 1873. Her family moved to Manitoba when she was seven years old. McClung began teaching after completing her education. She married Robert Wesley McClung in 1896.

In 1921, McClung was elected to the Alberta Legislature. Working with other women, together known as the Famous Five, she put forward a petition in 1927 to define the word "persons" in the British North America Act. This action helped women become more equal under the law. Nellie McClung died in Victoria, B.C., in 1951.

Clara Hawker (1873–1949)

Clara Hawker was born in 1873. During the war, she kept a diary of her experiences in school exercise books. Hawker had two sons serving in the Newfoundland Regiment.

In her diary, Hawker wrote down details of family life and events in the community that she thought her sons would enjoy reading about when the war was over. She also joined the Women's Patriotic Association, knitting socks and sewing shirts for Canadian soldiers overseas.

Hawker's diaries present a vivid picture of life at home for women during World War I. She was proud of her sons and missed them very much. Both sons were wounded, and one was sent home where he died of his wounds. Clara Hawker died in 1949. Her diaries, along with letters and postcards from her sons, are in the Carbonear Museum in Newfoundland.

Sir William Otter (1843–1929)

Sir William Otter fought in many campaigns, including the North-West Resistance of 1885 in Saskatchewan and the Second Boer War (1899–1902) in southern Africa. Otter retired from the military in 1910 at the rank of general.

Otter was born in Clinton, Ontario, in 1843. When he grew up, he became a part-time soldier and only joined the military full-time in 1883. He was a very strict commander, but his training methods helped prepare Canadian soldiers for war.

Otter was knighted in 1913. When World War I began, General Otter came out of retirement. He was put in charge of Canada's internment camps, which were located all around the country. After Sir Arthur Currie, Sir William Otter was only the second Canadian soldier to achieve the rank of general.

Canada's War

World War I was fought far away from Canada, but the conflict still affected people all over the country. All Canadians experienced the rationing, shortages, and tax increases brought about by the war. Across Canada, families had fathers, sons, or brothers serving overseas, many of whom either did not return or were wounded. At home, those men considered to be enemy aliens were interned in camps all over Canada. These men were torn from their families. War production took place in many different parts of the country, driving the economy.

During the war, some people were arrested for being spies.

By the Numbers

World War I was the most destructive war the world had ever seen. The war caused many changes in society, including a more important role for women, major changes to the economy, and a rise of Canada's international importance on the world stage.

Canada Before and After the War

DEBT	1914	1918
Canada	$544 million	$2 billion
Newfoundland	$30.5 million	$42 million

EMPLOYMENT	1914	1918
Employed women	600,000	1,200,00

CANADA'S ARMY	1914	1918
Full-time soldiers	3,100	620,000

MILITARY NURSES	1914	1917
Permanent	5	2,030
Reserve	57	203

The thousands of people interned in Canada's internment camps were treated according to international prisoner-of-war standards.

Statistics from the Home Front

$1.50 average daily payment to a soldier's family from the Canadian Patriotic Fund

$273,423 money distributed to **14,615** families from the Canadian Patriotic Fund in April **1915**

22,385 number of young men who served with Soldiers of the Soil to help farmers grow food

2,400 number of Niagara region women who picked fruit to help the war effort in **1918**

$53,084,863 money from mining exports in **1914**

92,686,291 wheat production by the bushel in **1913**; reached **150,342,037** bushels by **1918**

620,000 total Canadian soldiers who served during the war

424,000 Canadian soldiers who served overseas during World War I

2.9 KILOTONS amount of explosives on the *Mont Blanc* when it exploded in Halifax harbour

9,000 number of people injured in the Halifax Explosion

6,000 number of people left homeless by the Halifax Explosion

600 number of Imperial Munitions Board (IMB) factories by **1918**

289,000 number of IMB employees by **1919**, when it stopped operations

The War Comes to an End

By the time World War I finally ended in 1918, Canada's economy had greatly expanded, industries had been developed, and agricultural production had increased. There was a great feeling of patriotism. Canada had taken a large step toward becoming an important member of the global community of nations.

Canada had made a massive contribution to the Allied war effort and was in a position to demand a larger say in its own affairs after 1918. Canada signed the Treaty of Versailles separately from Great Britain and also joined the newly established League of Nations. Yet at home, Canada was deeply in debt, and both society and the workforce had been transformed. With the war over, many factories closed. The economy suffered. It suffered more when all the soldiers began returning home. These men needed work, but there often was no work. The war had also created deep divisions in society, and there was a sense of unrest throughout Canada.

The conscription crisis had created tension between English and French Canadians. In the west, farmers resented the government's policies, and the Progressive Party was formed. It was based in Alberta, Saskatchewan, Manitoba, and rural Ontario and won more seats than the Conservatives in the 1921 election. The party did not last long, but the New Democratic Party later adopted many of its ideas. People who had been in camps as enemy aliens distrusted the government. Labour unions had played an important role in the war effort and demanded greater rights for workers after 1918, which led to strikes. Less than a year after the war ended, the Winnipeg General Strike was the largest workers disturbance in Canadian history. On June 21, 1919, a riot resulted in two deaths and many injuries and arrests.

The government had intervened in the lives of ordinary Canadians during the management of the war effort. The measures undertaken helped form the basis of Canada's social welfare system. Women had been campaigning for the right to vote before 1914, but during the war, some of the provinces granted women the vote. As World War I drew to a close, women 21 and older were finally given the right to vote in federal elections and to stand for public office. Women had filled the jobs vacated by men fighting in Europe and had made a significant contribution to the war effort. Many of them did not keep these jobs when the war ended, but the role of women in Canadian society had changed as a result of World War I.

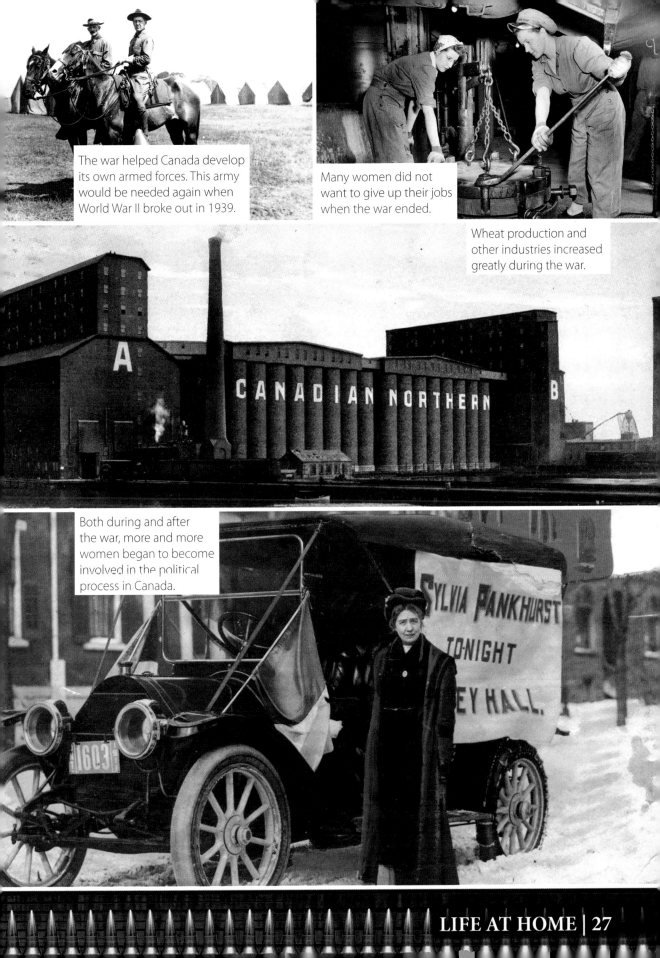

The war helped Canada develop its own armed forces. This army would be needed again when World War II broke out in 1939.

Many women did not want to give up their jobs when the war ended.

Wheat production and other industries increased greatly during the war.

CANADIAN NORTHERN

Both during and after the war, more and more women began to become involved in the political process in Canada.

SYLVIA PANKHURST TO-NIGHT EY HALL.

1603

Wartime Challenges

To support the military effort, rationing of certain items was introduced in Canada during World War I. Some foods, energy sources, and other supplies were sometimes not available or were severely restricted.

Using the Internet, books from your local library, and any other sources, research the challenges Canadian families faced in their daily lives during World War I.

FEED a FIGHTER
Eat only what you need —
Waste nothing —
That he and his family
may have enough

- How could you use resources efficiently and also avoid waste in your home?

- What kinds of things could you do to save energy?

- How could you ensure that you and your family had enough to eat?

- What adjustments could you make in your everyday diet to compensate for items that were unavailable or in short supply?

- What kinds of things could you do to help raise money for the war effort?

Draw a concept map or web based on your findings. Write a report based on your web or map.

Concept Web

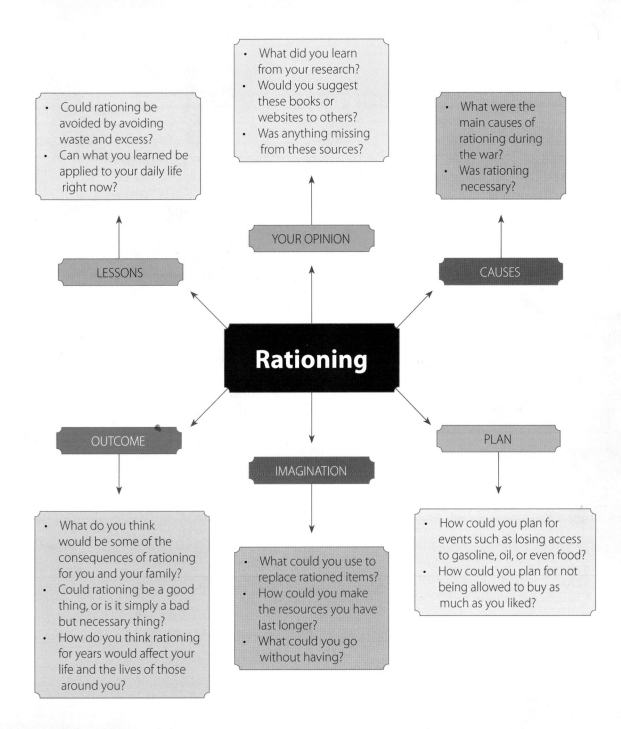

- What did you learn from your research?
- Would you suggest these books or websites to others?
- Was anything missing from these sources?

YOUR OPINION

- Could rationing be avoided by avoiding waste and excess?
- Can what you learned be applied to your daily life right now?

LESSONS

- What were the main causes of rationing during the war?
- Was rationing necessary?

CAUSES

Rationing

OUTCOME

- What do you think would be some of the consequences of rationing for you and your family?
- Could rationing be a good thing, or is it simply a bad but necessary thing?
- How do you think rationing for years would affect your life and the lives of those around you?

IMAGINATION

- What could you use to replace rationed items?
- How could you make the resources you have last longer?
- What could you go without having?

PLAN

- How could you plan for events such as losing access to gasoline, oil, or even food?
- How could you plan for not being allowed to buy as much as you liked?

Test Your Knowledge

1 When were most women age 21 and older given the right to vote in federal elections?

2 What was the population of Canada in 1914?

3 Who was the leader of the Opposition during the war?

4 How many aircraft were built in Canada during the war?

5 What was the IMB?

6 In what Canadian city were there riots over the conscription issue at Easter 1918?

7 How much money did the Canadian Patriotic Fund raise during the war?

8 How many people died in the Halifax Explosion?

9 Who was in charge of Canada's internment operation during World War I?

10 Name three food items that were taxed during World War I?

Answer Key
1. May 24, 1918 2. Almost 8 million 3. Sir Wilfrid Laurier 4. More than 2,600 5. The Imperial Munitions Board 6. Quebec City 7. Almost $50 million 8. 1,900 9. Sir William Otter 10. Tea, coffee, and sugar.

Further Resources

CHECK IT OUT!

www.warmuseum.ca/cwm/
exhibitions/guerre/home-e.aspx

www.canadaatwar.ca/page43.html

www.thecanadianencyclopedia.
com/articles/first-world-war-wwi

www.cbc.ca/history/
SECTIONSE1EP12CH2LE.html

Glossary

Canadian Patriotic Fund: a private organization that raised funds for soldiers and their families

civil liberties: rights that are protected by law, such as the freedom of speech and the right to a fair trial

colony: a country or area under the control of another country

conscription: mandatory enrolment in the armed forces

dominion: a self-governing territory of an empire

enemy aliens: citizens of enemy countries who are considered to be possible traitors

income tax: a tax placed by the government on the annual incomes of individuals and corporations

interned: confined during wartime

munitions: military equipment, especially ammunition

philanthropist: a person active in social welfare, often giving financial help to the poor or donating money to worthy causes

propaganda: media that is used to promote opinions and beliefs

ration: a fixed allowance for specific items, such as fuel and food

suffrage: the right to vote in elections

Treaty of Versailles: the 1919 agreement between the Allies and Germany that forced Germany to give up many of its territories and accept full responsibility for the war

U-boat: the name first given to German submarines in World War I

Unionists: political party comprising Conservatives and Liberals who supported conscription

Victory Bonds: government certificates that promise to repay borrowed funds by a particular date and at a fixed rate of interest

War Measures Act: a law that allowed the federal government to limit or completely suspend civil liberties to protect the country

Index